Sex With God Discussion Guide

A Workbook for Group Leaders

Suzanne DeWitt Hall
D. DeWitt Hall

DH Strategies

First Edition

ISBN: 978-1-7347427-1-8

Printed in the United States of America

CONTENTS

INTRODUCTION

Sex is one of the most powerful motivators of human behavior. It can be messy and disruptive, but can also be glorious and sublime. In an era of Christian deconstruction, many of us question the teachings of purity culture which formed our sexual ethic, and recognize the need to create a new one. *Sex With God* provides a tool for encouraging thought and conversation about topics of sexuality so readers can develop a new ethic.

Thank you for your willingness to lead a group through the devotional, and to facilitate that conversation. As the group study leader, your job is to prepare sacred space in which God's truth freely roams; a space where the Holy Spirit can speak revelation into the hearts and minds of attendees. Please understand that it is not your role to argue, convince, or be some sort of truth warrior. You are called simply to this:

To be a conduit which gives participants the freedom to speak, and which helps clear the way for the Holy Spirit to be heard.

We are in prayer for you and for your group's work together.

HOW TO USE THIS GUIDE

The first part of this guide will help you plan:

- Details like whether or not to serve snacks, how you'll manage time, and what supplies you'll want to have on hand.

- Your group's meeting schedule. A template is included which you can distribute to participants at the first meeting.

- The group's kickoff meeting.

- How each weekly session will be structured.

The second part of the guide is a collection of worksheets for use during weekly meetings:

- Topic summaries for you to present as a distillation of the session's overall focus.

- Daily Summaries which do the same thing for each daily reading included in the study session. Space is provided after each summary so you can jot down your own thoughts as you read the devotions.

- Points for Discussion pages containing questions for participants, which can be photocopied and distributed to study group members.

The guide concludes with a suggested format and questions for your final meeting.

Tips and Tricks

Snacks!

A hallmark of Jesus' ministry and the early church were people gathering around the table to hear the good news and break bread together. The act of feeding and receiving nourishment leads to connectedness. Consider having a simple snack at each meeting, along with cups and a pitcher of water. Ask participants about food allergies, and plan accordingly. When you've provided a snack for a few weeks, others are likely to offer to bring in a goody, which further helps people draw together because they are contributing to the feeding of both body and soul. If you do choose to include food in your study sessions, be sure to say yes to these offers.

Time Management

Your goal as facilitator is to encourage discussion, to draw out the quiet people in the group, and to charitably move the conversation out of the hands of over-sharers. But managing time can be a challenge, so here are a few tips:

- Although your study will have start and end times, keep in mind that the group will probably need at least five minutes to settle in and allow for everyone to arrive.

- As you reach the halfway point in the discussion questions, start keeping your eye on the clock. You may need to move things along more quickly in order to finish up on schedule.

- If you aren't great at time keeping, one of the participants may be. Let the group know you're committed to respecting their time, and that you'd appreciate help in paying attention to the clock.

- Alarms or timers on phones are useful. You can set one for 15 minutes before the end, and for 5 minutes before. Since alarms are impersonal, participants' feelings aren't hurt by nudges about needing to move forward.

Supplies

- Each week you'll distribute the discussion questions for the following week, however, be sure to have extra copies on the day of the meeting in case people forget to bring them.

- Have a few Bibles on hand for participants who want to refer to one during your time together.

- For snacks and drinks, plan on having a supply of small plates, napkins, utensils, cups, etc.

MEETING SCHEDULE

DATE	TOPIC	READINGS
	Kickoff Meeting	Introduction
	God's View of Sex	Days 1-10
	Practical Matters	Days 11-18
	How Not to Do It	Days 19-27
	Scandalous… or Not?	Days 28-36
	Proceed With Caution	Days 37-41
	Sacred Sexuality	Days 42-50
	Wrap-up Meeting	Conclusion

SUGGESTED KICKOFF MEETING FORMAT

Here's a suggested outline for your initial meeting.

1. Welcome participants and introduce yourself.

2. Cover logistics such as the location of bathrooms and other pertinent details.

3. Open with prayer.

4. Explain why you're holding the study. Offer a bit of your story as it relates to the topic.

5. Ask participants to introduce themselves and state why they decided to attend the study.

6. Explain the format of the study, and offer guidelines about how you want things to work if you have any (approach for sexual terminology, speaking by mutual invitation, method for managing time, etc.)

7. Request that people consider the group a sacred space for sharing vulnerable thoughts, and that personal insights remain confidential.

8. Read the *Introduction* together as a group, either silently or aloud, and then discuss the questions on the following page of this guide.

9. Hand out the next week's discussion questions.

10. Suggest that participants pray before they do each day's reading; that God would reveal what to focus on and how to respond.

11. Let participants know there are no right answers to the questions. Instead, they are meant to encourage thought to help fuel discussion.

12. Distribute the schedule of meeting dates, pointing out any weeks which need to be skipped due to holidays or other events. Let attendees know how long each meeting will last (one and a half hours is recommended).

13. Ask if there are any questions.

14. Close in prayer.

POINTS FOR DISCUSSION: KICKOFF MEETING

Read the introduction together as a group, either silently or aloud, and then discuss the following questions.

QUESTIONS

1. Is sex sacred and holy? Why or why not?

2. How do you think God feels about us considering this topic?

3. What should we make of the idea that Christianity begins with a woman conceiving a child?

4. Do you see desire as a holy thing? Have you ever associated sexuality with the divine?

5. What is your comfort level discussing sex and faith right now?

6. How important do you think this topic is for the church and society as a whole?

7. How equipped do you feel for discussing sex with friends, family, or members of your congregation?

Suggested Weekly Meeting Format

You're obviously free to run your book study any way you'd like, but here's a structure you might find helpful.

1. Open with prayer.

2. Present a high-level summary of the week's readings. (Weekly summaries are provided in this guide.)

3. Invite participants to offer reactions or revelations about the week as a whole.

4. Offer a summary of the first day's reading. (Daily summaries are also provided in this guide.)

5. Go through the first day's discussion questions, inviting participants to share their thoughts.

6. Repeat steps 4 and 5 for the remaining days.

7. Ask for concluding comments or questions.

8. Distribute the following week's discussion questions.

9. Close with prayer.

DISCUSSION MATERIALS

The pages which follow are pairs of materials for each topic area in the study:

- The first pages are an outline of the topic and the individual days within it. You can make notes for comments to offer the group, and use the summary text as an introduction for topics during group meetings.

- The subsequent pages are discussion questions which you can photocopy and distribute to group participants for the following week.

God's View of Sex

Topic Summary

The study begins by clarifying the pronouns which will be used for God, and then unfolds into 10 days of thought centering around the reality that God is love. Topics include the idea that sex is sacred, that it isn't dirty, that God's view is rarely binary, that pleasure is a good thing, that God loves bodies, that the wisdom of Solomon had room for thousands of loves, that God's burning desire is for every human, that their judgement is not like our judgement, and that the creation of the universe was essentially a cosmic orgasm.

Daily Summaries

Day 1: God is Love

The closing words in 1 John 4:7-8 ("God is love") are explored, including a look at what it means to *be* love, and how humans reflect being love through our sexuality.

Day 2: The Sacredness of Sexuality

The idea of sexual desire as a reflection of God's endless desire is examined, with an introduction to the concept of covenant as part of sacredness.

Day 3: Sex Isn't Dirty

A passage which highlight's the erotic intensity of the Song of Songs is presented, to stand in contrast to the idea that sex is dirty and that our desires are shameful.

Day 4: Non-Dualistic Sex

Philippians 4:4-7 is used to point out that God is in all things, that sex can be messy and complicated, and that black and white views are rarely places to find the divine.

Day 5: Pleasure is a Good Thing

The author asks why we are afraid of pleasure, and offers a passage from Psalm 16 to demonstrate God's desire for us to receive it.

Day 6: God Loves Bodies

The use of all five senses in the scriptures and Jesus' experience of those senses are described as illustrating God's love for our bodies and the desires we experience through them.

Day 7: The Slutty Wisdom of Solomon

A passage from 1 Kings is highlighted to ponder whether Solomon's wisdom (which coincided with his hundreds or thousands of partners) somehow reflects God's.

Day 8: God the Polyamorous Pansexual

The idea that God burns with passion for each and every human is explored.

Day 9: On Judging

Our tendency to judge other people's sex life is contrasted with the complexity of erotic encounters presented in scripture.

Day 10: Big Bang Indeed

The concept of God's creation of the universe through the Big Bang is unfolded.

POINTS FOR DISCUSSION: GOD'S VIEW OF SEX

Day 1: God is Love

The passage repeats "God is love" numerous times. What *is* love?

What are your experiences of love?

Day 2: The Sacredness of Sexuality

What do you think about the Big Bang as cosmic orgasm?

How does the beauty of God's desire for union manifest itself?

Day 3: Sex Isn't Dirty

Why do you think the Song of Songs is in the Bible?

The wisest person in Hebrew Scripture is thought to have written the Song of Songs. What might this tell us about wisdom?

Day 4: Non-Dualistic Sex

Why are we drawn to black and white thinking?

Has Philippians 4:4-7 been part of your faith experience? How have you used it?

Day 5: Pleasure is a Good Thing

In what do you find pleasure?

Can you envision pleasure as sacred?

Day 6: God Loves Bodies

How do you feel about your body?

Does God love your body? How do you know?

Day 7: The Slutty Wisdom of Solomon

What do you make of wisdom in the context of Solomon's love life?

How might Solomon's sexual reality have contributed to the content of the Song of Songs?

Day 8: God the Polyamorous Pansexual

Why didn't God condemn Solomon's embrace of so very many lovers?

How do you experience God's love for you?

Day 9: On Judging

What do you make of the author saying scripture is like the veil of a seductive dancer?

What spiritual or behavioral lines in the sand do you draw?

Day 10: Big Bang Indeed

What do you think of the idea that human orgasms are a reflection of God's initial creation of the universe?

If you had the ability to design a new being, which of your personality traits and characteristics would you build in?

Practical Matters

Topic Summary

This week's readings include the topic of consent, how to take it when a partner says "no," communication, focusing our awareness of touch, the concept of sex languages, the reality that sexual attraction isn't binary, the idea of equal access to orgasms, and an introduction to asexuality.

Daily Summaries

Day 11: Consent

The basics of consent are outlined and expanded to describe the less clear reality of how pressuring a partner can result in reluctant yesses.

Day 12: Nos are Okay

Being told "no" to a sexual advance can be frustrating or hurt our feelings. The author presents a way to transform that reaction into something more useful.

Day 13: Communication

The idea of communication as the way to manage sexual compatibility challenges is presented, along with an invitation to add God into the process.

Day 14: Intensity of Awareness

The author compares our tuning in to sensations during sex to the way we focus on individual instruments in a symphony or identify each blooming flavor which washes our tongues when we drink wine.

Day 15: Sex Languages

The idea of love languages is morphed to a system of mapping our sexual turn-ons and turn-offs.

Day 16: Sexual Attraction Isn't Binary

The complexity of sexual attraction is presented, along with the author's premise that being attracted to more kinds of people is actually more like God than being attracted to only one kind.

Day 17: Orgasms are for Everyone Who Wants Them

Differences in male versus female genital complexity is discussed along with the relative rareness of women's orgasms in heterosexual couples.

Day 18: Asexuality

An overview of asexuality is presented in the form of a donut analogy. Communication about levels of sexual desire is encouraged, and readers are reminded that lack of attraction or desire does not make a person broken.

POINTS FOR DISCUSSION: PRACTICAL MATTERS

Day 11: Consent

What are your experiences of saying yes but not meaning yes?

Have you ever thought of consent as a sacred interaction?

Day 12: Nos are Okay

How do you feel when a sexual advance is turned down?

How can you turn that deflation into something positive?

Day 13: Communication

How easy has it been for you to talk about sex with intimate partners?

How can you involve the divine in this communication process?

Day 14: Intensity of Awareness

What gets in the way of our tuning in to the individual elements of music, wine, and intimate touch?

Why would intensifying our awareness as described improve our enjoyment?

Day 15: Sex Languages

How much do you think people talk about these things with their partners?

What stops this kind of conversation? What could encourage it?

Day 16: Sexual Attraction Isn't Binary

What do you think about the idea that being non-binary is more like God than existing at any particular pole?

Is shame about our attraction emotionally or spiritually useful? Why or why not?

Day 17: Orgasms are for Everyone Who Wants Them

What is your comfort level in talking about orgasms?

How deeply have you considered this issue for yourself and for your partner?

Day 18: Asexuality

What was your understanding of asexuality up until today? Has it shifted after reading the reflection?

How can love build a bridge between an asexual person and an allosexual person (one who *does* experience sexual attraction)?

How Not to Do It

Topic Summary

The readings from this week focus on purity culture, shame, using others, sex as a drug, abuse, forced celibacy, body image, adultery, and people having sex at too young an age.

Daily Summaries

Day 19: Purity Culture

A list of some of the negative impacts of purity culture is presented, along with a corresponding list of corrective thoughts.

Day 20: Shame

The author points out the corrosive effect of shame, and urges us to lay our self-judgements about the past down.

Day 21: Using Others

The reality of every human being as a carrier of the divine is explored, along with a call for us to honor that reality in our sexual activity.

Day 22: Sex as a Drug

The problem of people using sex to numb the difficulties of life or areas of brokenness is discussed.

Day 23: Abuse

Varying kinds of abuse are described, and readers are urged to seek healing from it if they've been abused, and repentance of it if they've been an abuser.

Day 24: Forced Celibacy

Passages about celibacy as a spiritual gift from 1 Corinthians 7 are presented, as a reminder that celibacy shouldn't be used as punishment for being gay or for any other reason.

Day 25: Unrealistic Body Image

The author offers insight into how to help your beloved (or yourself) overcome negative emotions related to body image.

Day 26: Adultery

Varying scenarios in which adultery can take place are examined, along with the potential for good to sometimes result through the brokenness.

Day 27: Starting Too Young

A vision of how to talk to young people about sex is introduced, in an effort to help them experience fewer of the problems which can result from engaging too early.

Day 19: Purity Culture

Do you think referring to purity culture as "rape culture in its Sunday best" is valid? Why or why not?

How has purity culture impacted your life or the life of those around you?

Day 20: Shame

Why is shame problematic?

What tactics can be employed to combat shame and put it behind you?

Day 21: Using Others

We are a mix of body and spirit, each offering demands and desires. What do you think God has in mind for us through these often conflicting realities? How might this process of balance be a means of achieving holiness?

What would it look like to stop in the throes of passion and honor the God-ness of the object of your desires?

Day 22: Sex as a Drug

Could society's public preoccupation with sex be a symptom of a culture-wide desire for numbness?

Where is the line between sex as a healthy engagement in comfort and sex as a compulsion?

Day 23: Abuse

If you know someone who is being abused or has been in the past, please encourage them to get help. The *Rape, Abuse & Incest National Network* (www.rainn.org) offers resources including the *National Sexual Assault Hotline* (800-656-HOPE).

What advice could you offer a friend to help break the control an abuser has over them?

What can we do when raising and training young people to help reduce abuse?

Day 24: Forced Celibacy

Have you known anyone who chose to be celibate? Why did they choose it?

Look at the last line of Paul's words to the church in Corinth. Should gay or lesbian people be exempt from these instructions? Why or why not?

Day 25: Unrealistic Body Image

Do you think body image impacts the sexes differently?

How can you help your partner or yourself feel better about their/your body without using platitudes?

Day 26: Adultery

What constitutes adultery?

What do you think God's judgement is like?

Day 27: Starting Too Young

How were you introduced to the topic of sex by adults? What was your reaction when it occurred?

What kind of conversations do you wish you'd had when you were young, to help you develop a healthier view of sex?

Scandalous... or Not?

Topic Summary

This week's reading centers around topics which are frequently viewed as scandalous, including premarital sex, infidelity, masturbation, fantasies and role playing, bisexuality, polyamory, pornography, BDSM, and sex work.

Daily Summaries

Day 28: Sex Before Marriage

The idea of the sacrament of marriage as being performed by the couple rather than by a priest or pastor is presented, and the concept of the kind of relationship God desires for sexual covenant is described.

Day 29: Infidelity

The complexity of infidelity is explored, along with ways in which it is sometimes used to break prison doors.

Day 30: Masturbation

Paul's words in the first letter to the church in Corinth are presented as the setting for a discussion about masturbation as a sacred way to endure temptation.

Day 31: Fantasies and Role Playing

A reminder is offered that fantasizing about others often reduces them to objects, but the author suggests that there are ways to fantasize without doing so.

Day 32: Bisexuality

Stereotypes about bisexuals are debunked, and passages describing the love between David and Johnathan in first and second Samuel are evaluated.

Day 33: Polyamory

The topic of polyamory is revisited, with the conclusion that while it's possible for some humans to be able to love multiple partners with the depth of intimacy God desires, it is rare.

Day 34: Pornography

The author presents pornography as a form of objectification of others, and therefore inherently problematic, but invites readers to share their thoughts on how it can be something else.

Day 35: BDSM

An overview of bondage and discipline as part of sadomasochistic sexual practices is provided, along with the author's perception that desiring to inflict or receive degradation and pain is not a form of love.

Day 36: Sex Work

Some of the problems related to sex work are discussed, and the author suggests that humans are not things to be purchased.

Day 28: Sex Before Marriage

What aspects of getting married bring about the kind of unitive covenant God desires? What aspects do not?

How does sex become godly?

Day 29: Infidelity

Is your view of life, sex, and faith more black and white now than it was five years ago? Is it less? What contributed to the shift, if one occurred?

Is it possible to make a relationship infidelity proof?

Day 30: Masturbation

Can masturbation be physically, mentally, and even spiritually beneficial?

How do you think we should talk about masturbation with young people?

Day 31: Fantasies and Role Playing

How do you react to the idea of imagining God making love to you?

Can you envision a way in which fantasies and/or role playing could make your sex life more intimate and sacred (even without a partner)?

Day 32: Bisexuality

How do you view the ardor of David and Johnathan's relationship as unfolded in the highlighted scripture passages?

What are your thoughts about the idea that bisexuals more closely mirror God than heterosexuals?

Day 33: Polyamory

What are your views on polyamory?

What qualities would someone need for truly intimate and sacred polyamorous unions?

Day 34: Pornography

What do people get from pornography?

Is there a way to bring those things into a sacred intimate relationship, with your spouse or yourself, without the objectification which is inherent in pornography?

Day 35: BDSM

Why does BDSM excite some people? What do they get from it?

Can you get those things in a sacred, intimate, painless, sexual interaction?

Day 36: Sex Work

What leads someone to engage in sex work? What draws someone to seek out a sex worker?

What would the world need to be like to make sex work an historical artifact?

PROCEED WITH CAUTION

TOPIC SUMMARY

This week's study focuses on some warnings about sex, including the lie of desirability, sex being like epoxy, soul ties, sex versus intimacy, and the reality that sex can't fix you.

DAILY SUMMARIES

Day 37: The Lie of Desirability

The author addresses our problematic tendency to measure ourselves against a social construct of sexual desirability.

Day 38: Sex is Like Epoxy

Mark 10:8's statement about the two becoming one flesh is presented as a warning, and the chemistry of coupling is discussed.

Day 39: Soul Ties

The idea that souls connect through sexual activity is examined, along with a few images of what those connections can look like.

Day 40: Sex Versus Intimacy

Jesus' beautiful prayer urging oneness in John 17 is used as a model for the kind of intimacy God desires for our sexual relationships.

Day 41: Sex Can't Fix You

The problem of people thinking sex will make them whole is evaluated, and a caution issued that engaging in sex for this purpose might even make things worse.

Points for Discussion: Proceed With Caution

Day 37: The Lie of Desirability

How important is feeling desirable to you?

What sorts of problems does a focus on desirability cause?

How can we battle the cultural focus on desirability in our own hearts and in discussion with young people?

Day 38: Sex is Like Epoxy

What are your thoughts on the Mark passage (10:8)?

Have you ever experienced what is described: temporarily feeling emotion for someone which you later realized was simply afterglow? What made you conclude it wasn't real?

What traits would you like to see in a person with whom you become powerfully bonded?

Day 39: Soul Ties

Do you still feel connections to past sexual partners? If yes, how do these connections impact you today?

What do you make of the idea that connections exist both inside and outside of time?

You've probably heard quotes about "the ties that bind." What ties bind us together?

Day 40: Sex Versus Intimacy

What strikes you about Jesus' prayer in John 17:20-23?

What does the kind of intimacy God desires look like?

How are sex and intimacy different? What does it take to have both in a relationship?

Day 41: Sex Can't Fix You

Have you known anyone who seeks sexual relationships as a way to escape their brokenness?

What kinds of brokenness do people try to fix through sex?

What advice would you give someone who is using sex to try to fix themself?

SACRED SEXUALITY

TOPIC SUMMARY

The readings for our final week circle back to where we started: the concept of sacred sexuality. Topics included monogamy, the cord of three strands, the concept of namaste, the need to escape our egos, the dance of giving and receiving, the issue of soul mates, orgasm as a "little death," becoming comfortable with our inability to fully know, and sacred touch.

DAILY SUMMARIES

Day 42: Monogamy

Monogamy has been preached as the Christian norm, but the model is being questioned as part of the deconstruction process sweeping the faithful. The author suggests that for the majority of people, it's the relationship structure which works best for deep intimacy.

Day 43: A Cord of Three

The idea of inviting God into our sexual encounters is presented, centering around the scriptural premise that a cord of three strands is not easily broken.

Day 44: Namaste

Several scripture passages offer insight into the reality that we are temples of the Holy Spirit, and the author describes how the separate (though never really separate) parts of the Spirit are reunited during sex.

Day 45: Escaping the Ego

The way our brains filter and diminish reality is explored, along with the promise of what sex could be like if we're able to turn off the ego-driven voices in our heads.

Day 46: The Dance of Giving and Receiving

Masculine versus feminine forms of spirituality are described, and readers are encouraged to try to be open and receptive in our faith lives and our sexuality.

Day 47: Bashert

The reading begins with a passage describing an idea from Jewish mysticism about souls being separated at birth and then reunited again in marriage. The author urges us to embrace the concept of life as a journey of becoming fully ourselves, and to find partners who help us do that.

Day 48: Le Petit Mort

The idea of orgasm being called "the little death" is explored, because of its combination of the halting of active awareness and euphoria.

Day 49: Knowing and Unknowing

The author suggests that the richness of awareness which comes from touch and sexual intimacy creates a kind of knowing which is deeper than intellectual knowledge of our beloved partners.

Day 50: Sacred Touch

Scripture passages about the power which goes out through touch are presented, along with the idea that we are similarly able to push out the power of the Spirit in touch during lovemaking.

Day 42: Monogamy

What are the benefits and downsides of monogamy versus polyamory?

Can you imagine yourself able to manage multiple partners where there is deep love and true intimacy? Why or why not?

Day 43: A Cord of Three

Have you ever felt the kind of experiential rather than intellectual knowing described in the opening paragraphs?

How do you feel about the idea of actively inviting God into lovemaking?

Day 44: Namaste

What do you think about the author's description of the Spirit within and outside of each partner merging?

What would it look like for the God in you to see, greet, and unite with the God in another?

Day 45: Escaping the Ego

What do you think about the idea of our brains being "diminishers of reality"?

How do we escape the glorious cages of our brains during lovemaking?

Day 46: The Dance of Giving and Receiving

How might this view of sexual offering and opening transform an assertive, outwardly thrusting sexuality?

What would a sexual dance with God be like?

Day 47: Bashert

Who are you when you are being more of yourself? What does that "moreness" look like?

How can you be the best possible bashert for your partner, or even for yourself?

Day 48: Le Petit Mort

What do you think of the idea of orgasm as a "coming attractions" trailer for existence beyond this one?

What would everyday life be like if you could capture the euphoric peace which comes after orgasm and take it out when you need it? Is it possible to do this?

Day 49: Knowing and Unknowing

Have you experienced the richness of knowing beyond intellectual understanding? What was/is it like?

What are the benefits of accepting there is an impenetrable space between you and God, your partner, and even yourself?

Day 50: Sacred Touch

How important is touch within the act of lovemaking?

What is your response to the concept of transmitting the Holy Spirit's energy during lovemaking?

Suggested Wrap-up Meeting Format

Your group has worked their way through *Sex With God*, gotten to know each other a whole lot better, and explored the topic of sexuality in a way they haven't before. All of these things are worthy of celebration! If it fits your style, consider holding a potluck at the final meeting, so everyone can let their hair down a bit, break bread together a final time, and share their conclusions about the study.

Here's an outline for how you might want to run this last get together:

1. Gather, pray, and eat (if you do decide to hold a potluck).

   Participating in your discussion group will have built community between members. While eating, people can simply enjoy each other's company and chat.

2. As dessert is served, ask for thoughts about the overall experience of the study.

3. Discuss the questions on the next page.

4. Thank participants for their candor, thoughtfulness, and honoring of the sacred space the group has represented.

5. Close in prayer.

POINTS FOR DISCUSSION: CONCLUDING MEETING

QUESTIONS

From the Conclusion:

- In what ways does the love you create affect not only you and your partner, but also the world?

- Do you think there will be sex in heaven?

General questions:

- Has your comfort level with discussing sex and faith increased after reading this book?

- In what ways have your views about sexuality shifted since we began the study?

- How equipped do you feel for discussing sex with friends, family, or members of your congregation?

- What actions could be taken within churches to help the faithful renew their understanding of sex and faith?

www.ingramcontent.com/pod-product-compliance
Lightning Source LLC
Chambersburg PA
CBHW081232020426
42331CB00012B/3147